THE BEGINNER'S GUIDE TO
A PLANT-BASED DIET

Use the Newest 3 Weeks Plant-Based Diet Meal Plan to Reset & Energize Your Body. Easy, Healthy and Whole Foods Recipes to Kick-Start a Healthy Eating.

ISBN 9781726126038

Brandon Hearn © 2018

Table of Contents

INTRODUCTION

A plant-based diet is all about celebrating and enjoying the foods that naturally fuel our bodies and are minimally processed. By improving your nutrition, you can improve your health, which is exactly what the plant-based diet is about. Don't dramatically change your diet without consulting your doctor to make sure that here will be no medical issues, such as problems with medications you may currently be on. You should also gradually change to the plant-based diet if you are a heavy meat eater.

It's that simple and I like to keep things that way. Yet not every plant-based diet is the same. You can make it *your* lifestyle and adjust it as you see fit.

You should feel energized because of the foods you eat, never lethargic or drained. Our bodies are incredible machines and the foods we eat are what help maintain and protect our awesomeness. That is what the plant-based lifestyle is all about.

That's all there is to it, but let's break it down a little further.

WHAT YOU'LL BE EATING

You'll be eating the following.

- **Starchy Vegetables:** This includes all kinds of potatoes, including sweet potatoes, legumes, which is all kinds of lentils and beans, whole corn, root vegetables and quinoa.
- **Non-Starchy Vegetables:** This includes your leafy greens, broccoli, eggplant, tomatoes, broccoli and more.
- **Whole Grains:** This includes things such as brown rice, oats, whole wheat and more.
- **Fruits:** All fruits are included if they're found in nature. This doesn't include juice or dried fruits.
- **Spices:** You can use all spices
- **Beverages:** Your beverages are limited on this diet. You can drink unsweetened plant "milks", decaffeinated coffee, decaffeinated tea and water.
- **Omega 3 Sources:** Your omega 3 sources are flax seed and chia seeds.

EAT THESE SPARINGLY

These are foods that you can have once in a while, but you should eat them sparingly.

- **Nuts:** The nuts you can eat sparingly are almonds, cashews, walnuts and peanuts.
- **Seeds:** The seeds you can eat sparingly are sesame, pumpkin and sunflower.
- Dried Fruit
- Coconut
- Avocado
- **Added Sweetener:** Use maple syrup, fruit juice concentrate and natural sugars sparingly
- **Beverages:** You can have caffeinated tea and coffee occasionally as well as the occasional alcoholic drink.
- **Refined Protein:** You can have refined soy and wheat protein sparingly
- **Tofu, Wheat Gluten Protein & Soy Protein Isolate**

THE BASICS

There is no portion control, no carb counting and no calorie counting with this diet plan. You can eat when you're hungry, and you can eat until you get full. Simply make sure that you choose food from the right categories. Of course, there are going to be exceptions that you'll need to make occasionally. You need to be sure that you aren't eating too often from your sparingly food category for example.

CHOOSE THE ONE FOR YOU

You can choose the plant-based diet for you! Here are some of the most common plant-based diets out there.

- **Veganism:** This is a diet that includes legumes, fruits, grains, vegetables, nuts and seeds, but you'll not be able to eat any food that's sourced from animals.
- **Raw Veganism:** This is a diet that includes uncooked and some dehydrated foods.
- **Vegetarianism:** This is a diet that consists of legumes, vegetables, nuts and fruit. You can include eggs and dairy in this diet, but you aren't allowed meat.
- **Fruitarianism:** This is a vegan diet that primarily involves fruit, but you should not use this if you are diabetic.
- **Ovo-lacto Vegetarianism:** This encourages that you eat eggs and dairy along with your fruit and vegetables.
- **Ovo Vegetarianism:** This is where you are allowed to eat eggs with your fruits and vegetables, but you still can't have dairy.
- **Lacto Vegetarianism:** This allows you to have dairy but no eggs with your fruits and vegetables.
- **Semi-Vegetarianism:** This is a mostly vegetarian diet with the occasional time that you can have meat.
- **Pescatarian:** This is a semi-vegetarian diet that allows you to have dairy, eggs, shellfish and fish.
- **Macrobiotic Diet:** This diet highlights whole grains, beans, miso soup, sea vegetables, vegetables, and naturally processed foods. This can be done with or without seafood and other animal products.

TIPS FOR THIS DIET

Here are some tips to get you started so you can stick to this diet with ease!

LOOK FOR MILK ALTERNATIVES

There are many non-dairy milk alternatives out there. There is coconut, cashew, Brazil nut, rice, almond and even hempseed milk substitutes out there. Most can be used in equal measurements, especially in baking. Just make sure you're using their unsweetened versions. The best is that most of these milks are rich in calcium so you won't be missing out.

LOOK FOR EGG ALTERNATIVES

You can also replace eggs in recipes. You can use six tablespoons of water with three tablespoons of chia seeds or ground flaxseeds. Just soak them for five to ten minutes so that the mixture becomes gelatinous. You can also use a quarter cup of pureed banana or a quarter cup of applesauce depending on the recipe. Each one of these is the equivalent of a single egg.

1/4 Cup Applesauce   1/2 Mashed Banana   Commercial Egg Replacer

1 Tbsp Vinegar + tsp Baking Soda   1 Tbsp Ground Flax Seed+ 3 tbsp Water

INSTEAD OF AN EGG

1/4 Cup Silken Tofu   1/4 Cup Soy Yogurt

LOOK FOR CHEESE ALTERNATIVES

There isn't a substitute for cheese, but the plant world does have soft and creamy textures that can take the place of cheese. It does make a small change in the taste of the dish, but it isn't too bad. The most popular replacements are soaked and blended cashews, sliced avocado, sprouted soft organic tofu, and nutritional yeast.

LOOK FOR MEAT ALTERNATIVES

For a rich, heart texture that will help to fill you up there is beans, Portobello mushrooms, tempeh, and tofu. Each of these are chewy and hearty, and they can be marinated to get different flavors. You can also use these for chili, stews, and burgers or can be served baked.

BE CAREFUL EATING OUT

It can be hard to dine out when you're trying to enjoy a plant-based diet. However, there are many restaurants that offer vegan options, so try to look for one in advance. Just realize that you'll need to minimize the number of times you eat out. However, if you need to go out then check out the menu online before you arrive. Look for dishes that are low in fat and full of vegetables, and then look for grilled, baked and steamed options. Try to avoid any dishes that are fried, rich, creamy or crispy. Just don't be shy about asking for a different salad dressing or side dish either. Make sure sauces and cheeses are left out too. If there's bread, ask for whole wheat. If there is rice, ask for brown rice.

PURGE YOUR KITCHEN

It's best that you get rid of any temptation that's in your kitchen and calling you name if you're trying to start a plant-based diet. It's not good to have unhealthy foods in front of you or you're bound to give in.

PLAN YOUR MEALS

Luckily this book comes with a meal plan that will help you to stick to your first three weeks of your diet. However, you may want to stick to planning your meals for the first few months if you find yourself struggling.

EIGHT FOOD BASED MISTAKES

In this chapter, you'll learn the eight common foods that are mistaken for plant-based ones. Avoid these if you want to stay on your plant-based diet.

BREAD

Most bread has milk products, so they're not plant based breads. However, you can make some plant-based breads if you're really missing sliced bread. It'll just take a little more work.

SOUP STOCK

Remember that even "mock" chicken stocks can contain a small amount of animal products or animal fat. This includes vegetarian stocks, so be careful! Don't just grab the bouillon either. It's safer to just make your own.

PASTA

Eggs are an essential component to pasta, so it's important you buy only dried pasta. Make sure that it's made of whole grains and water.

ORANGE JUICE

Most orange juice contains traces of fish oil. While this is healthy for you, it may violate your plant-based diet depending on which one you use.

GRANOLA

This is usually made of dried fruits, nuts, seeds and raw grains. However, they are often sweetened and can contain butter. It's best to make your own.

NON-DAIRY CREAMER

These creamers may not include milk, but they do often include milk products such as sodium caseinate which is a milk protein. It's better to look for vegan friendly creamers.

DAIRY-FREE CHEESE

There can be soy, nut, or even rice based "cheeses" that are labeled non-dairy, but they can include whey protein or casin. It's better to go for the vegan label when you're looking for a cheese substitute.

VEGGIE SAUSAGES & BURGERS

There is usually a small amount of eggs or milk to these products, so they're not completely plant based. They can also contain a lot of soy, so be careful which ones you get. However, you can make your own if you want to be sure what's going in it.

BASIC SHOPPING LIST

While you'll find an ingredient every once in a while, you just have to have for a recipe, here is a basic shopping list that will help you to get started! Starting a new diet is difficult, but when you know how to shop, it becomes much easier.

FRESH FRUITS!

You'll want to get some fresh fruit for this plant-based diet. Here are a few budget friendly options to get you started that you'll find useful for the recipes in this book. Remember that you can buy fruit in bulk at many local farmer markets.

- Strawberries
- Cantaloupe
- Blueberries
- Kiwi
- Mango
- Peaches
- Pears
- Oranges
- Apples
- Honeydew

FRESH VEGETABLES!

While you'll have fruit occasionally, a plant-based diet is very vegetable heavy. It's even easier to find vegetables at a reasonable price. Once again, you can check a local farmer's market, go to your nearest grocery store or even find a whole foods store that offers bulk buys.

- Leafy Greens (Kale, Spinach, Parsley, Bok Choy and Lettuce are the Cheapest)
- Eggplant
- Tomatoes
- Cauliflower
- Bell Pepper (All Colors, but Green is usually cheaper)
- Squash (Butternut, Zucchini & Spaghetti Squash is Cheapest)
- Olives
- Okra
- Avocado
- Onions

SOME EXTRAS

You'll find that you need more than just fruits and vegetables for your plant-based diet. Remember to stock up on the following.

- Rolled Oats
- Flaxseed
- Chia Seeds (These can be found online for cheaper than most grocery stores)
- Quinoa
- Lentils
- Beans (Uncooked is cheaper than canned)
- Sweet Potatoes
- Coconut Flour
- Almond Flour
- Milk Alternatives (Almond, Soy or Coconut milk are cheapest.
- Tofu
- Oils (Olive Oil or Coconut Oil is both cheap, healthy options)

HERBS & SPICES

You'll want to flavor your food, and to do that we turn to herbs and spices. Besides just salt and pepper, here are a few must haves!

- Parsley
- Basil
- Cilantro
- Garlic
- Ginger
- Curry Powder
- Red Pepper Flakes
- Paprika

21 DAY MEAL PLAN

Here's an easy twenty-one-day meal plan to follow with the recipes in this book!

DAY 1

Breakfast: Avocado Breakfast Bowl
Lunch: Baked Okra & Tomato
Dinner: Tofu Poke

DAY 2

Breakfast: Mango Smoothie
Lunch: Avocado & Radish Salad
Dinner: Simple Chili

DAY 3

Breakfast: Vegetable Hash
Lunch: Mediterranean Wrap
Dinner: Tomato Gazpacho

DAY 4

Breakfast: Berry & Cauliflower Smoothie
Lunch: Quinoa with Nectarine Slaw
Dinner: Sushi Bowl

DAY 5

Breakfast: Fruity Oatmeal
Lunch: Parsley Salad
Dinner: Simple Chili

DAY 6

Breakfast: Chia Seed Smoothie
Lunch: Red Lentil Soup
Dinner: Dijon Maple Burgers

DAY 7

Breakfast: Quinoa & Chocolate Bowl
Lunch: Watercress & Blood Orange Salad
Dinner: Tofu & Asparagus Stir Fry

DAY 8

Breakfast: Flaxseed Porridge
Lunch: Corn & Black Bean Salad
Dinner: Pesto & Tomato Quinoa

DAY 9

Breakfast: Breakfast Cereal
Lunch: Summer Chickpea Salad
Dinner: Fried Pineapple Rice

DAY 10

Breakfast: Granola
Lunch: Mac & "Cheese"
Dinner: Sesame Bok Choy

DAY 11

Breakfast: Fruit Salad
Lunch: Thai Squash Soup
Dinner: Cauliflower Steaks

DAY 12

Breakfast: Pumpkin Chia Smoothie
Lunch: Butter Bean Hummus
Dinner: Grilled Eggplant Steaks

DAY 13

Breakfast: Walnut Porridge
Lunch: Olive & Fennel Salad
Dinner: Stuffed Bell Pepper

DAY 14

Breakfast: Green Mango Smoothie
Lunch: Red Lentil Soup
Dinner: Black Bean Burgers

DAY 15

Breakfast: Vegetable Hash
Lunch: Spinach & Orange Salad
Dinner: Tofu Saag

DAY 16

Breakfast: Eggplant Hash Browns
Lunch: White Bean & Spinach Soup
Dinner: Vegetable Stir Fry

DAY 17

Breakfast: Flaxseed & Blueberry Porridge
Lunch: Zucchini & Lemon Salad
Dinner: Ratatouille

DAY 18

Breakfast: Avocado & Strawberry Bowl
Lunch: Black Eyed Pea Stew
Dinner: Fried Pineapple Rice

DAY 19

Breakfast: Coconut & Strawberry Bars
Lunch: Mediterranean Wrap
Dinner: Sesame Bok Choy

DAY 20

Breakfast: Flaxseed Pancakes
Lunch: Quinoa & Nectarine Slaw
Dinner: Stuffed Bell Pepper

DAY 21

Breakfast: Kiwi Slushie
Lunch: Parsley Salad
Dinner: Tofu & Asparagus Stir Fry

BREAKFAST RECIPES

Here are some breakfast recipes to get your day started right.

FLAXSEED & BLUEBERRY PORRIDGE

Serves: 2
Calories: 405
Protein: 10 Grams
Fat: 34 Grams
Carbs: 12 Grams

Ingredients:

- 1 Cup Almond Milk
- ¼ Cup Coconut Flour
- 1 Teaspoon Cinnamon
- ¼ Cup Flaxseed, Ground
- 1 Teaspoon Vanilla Extract
- 10 Drops Stevia
- Pinch Sea Salt

Garnish:

- 1 Ounces Coconut, Shaved
- 2 Tablespoon Pumpkin Seeds
- 2 Tablespoons Almond Butter
- 2 Ounces Blueberries

Directions:

1. Heat your almond milk in a saucepan over low heat, whisking in your coconut flour, salt, cinnamon and flaxseed
2. Once it bubbles, add in your vanilla and stevia
3. Remove from heat, garnishing as desired.

AVOCADO & STRAWBERRY BOWL

Serves: 1
Calories: 140
Protein: 2 Grams
Fat: 10 Grams
Carbs: 5 Grams

Ingredients:

- 1 Cup Strawberries
- 1 Cup Avocado, Peeled & Pitted
- 1 Teaspoon Lime
- Stevia to Taste
- Pinch Sea Salt

Directions:

1. Blend all ingredients until smooth.

COCONUT & STRAWBERRY BARS

Serves: 2

Time: 4 Hours 10 Minutes

Calories: 294

Protein: 3 Grams

Fat: 28 Grams

Carbs: 4 Grams

Ingredients:

- 1 Tablespoon Coconut Oil
- 1 Cup Strawberries, Chopped
- 16 Ounces Coconut Butter, Melted
- 1 Teaspoon Stevia
- ¼ Cup Coconut Flakes, Unsweetened

Directions:

1. Mix your stevia, oil, and butter together, transferring it to a prepared baking dish.
2. Add your strawberries and coconut, and then refrigerate for four hours. Chop into bars.

AVOCADO BREAKFAST BOWL

Serves: 1
Time: 5 Minutes
Calories: 562
Protein: 8 Grams
Fat: 52 Grams
Carbs: 7 Grams

Ingredients:

- 2 Tablespoons Tahini
- 1 Carrot, Shredded
- 1 Avocado, Halved & Pit Removed

Sauce:

- Sea Salt to Taste
- ¼ Cup Olive Oil
- 1 Teaspoon Ginger, Fresh & Grated
- 1 Tablespoon Poppy Seeds
- ¼ Cup Lemon Juice

Directions:

1. Start by whisking all of your sauce ingredients together, and then mix all other ingredients together.
2. Drizzle your sauce over your bowl before serving.

COCONUT & STRAWBERRY SMOOTHIE

Serves: 1
Time: 10 Minutes
Calories: 278
Protein: 14 Grams
Fat: 2 Grams
Carbs: 57 Grams

Ingredients:

- 1 Cup Strawberries, Frozen & Thawed Slightly
- 1 Ripe Banana, Sliced & Frozen
- ½ Cup Coconut Milk, Light
- ½ Cup Greek Yogurt, Plain
- 1 Tablespoon Chia Seeds
- 1 Teaspoon Lime juice, Fresh
- 4 Ice Cubes

Directions:

1. Blend everything together until smooth, and serve immediately.

FLAXSEED PANCAKES

Serves: 1
Time: 15 Minutes
Calories: 309
Protein: 13.4 Grams
Fat: 27.1 Grams
Carbs: 5 Grams

Ingredients:

- 3 Tablespoons Water
- 2 Tablespoons Flaxseeds
- Pinch Sea Salt
- 1 ½ Tablespoons Coconut Oil
- ½ Scoop Vanilla Vegan Powder
- ¼ Teaspoon Baking Powder

Directions:

1. Mix a tablespoon of flaxseeds with water, and then mix in your oil.
2. Mix your baking powder, protein powder, flax seed and salt together in a bowl.
3. Add your wet and dry ingredients together, and then heat a nonstick pan over medium heat.
4. Scoop batter into your pan, cooking for five minutes. Flip cooking for two minutes on the other side. Repeat until you've finished all your batter.

PUMPKIN CHIA SMOOTHIE

Serves: 1
Time: 5 Minutes
Calories: 726
Protein: 5.5 Grams
Fat: 69.8 Grams
Carbs: 15 Grams

Ingredients:

- 3 Tablespoons Pumpkin Puree
- 1 Tablespoon MCT Oil
- ¾ Cup Coconut Milk, Full Fat
- ½ Avocado, Fresh
- 1 Teaspoon Vanilla, Pure
- ½ Teaspoon Pumpkin Pie Spice

Directions:

1. Combine all ingredients together until blended.

EGGPLANT HASH BROWNS

Serves: 8
Time: 20 Minutes
Calories: 100
Protein: 2.42 Grams
Fat: 6.4 Grams
Carbs: 8 Grams

Ingredients:

- 1 Eggplant, Peeled, Cubed & Salted
- 2 Tablespoons Coconut Oil
- 1 Red Onion, Diced
- 2 Red Bell Peppers, Seeded & Diced
- 4 Cloves Garlic, Minced
- ¼ Cup Almonds, Slivered & Toasted
- ¼ Cup Mint Leaves, Fresh
- ½ Cup Sundried Tomatoes, Drained & Chopped
- ½ Teaspoon Coriander Seeds
- ¼ Teaspoon Cayenne Pepper
- ½ Teaspoon Cinnamon
- Sea Salt & Black Pepper to Taste

Directions:

1. Start by heating oil in a skillet, searing your bell pepper and eggplant, cooking for three minutes. Make sure to stir occasionally.
2. Add in your onion and garlic, cooking for two minutes.
3. Toss in your mint leaves, almonds and tomatoes. Make sure to heat all the way through, and then add in the rest of your ingredients.

CANTALOUPE SMOOTHIE BOWL

Serves: 2
Time: 5 Minutes
Calories: 135
Protein: 3 Grams
Fat: 1 Gram
Carbs: 32 Grams

Ingredients:

- ¾ Cup carrot Juice
- 4 Cps Cantaloupe, Frozen & Cubed
- Mellon Balls or Berries to Serve
- Pinch Sea Salt

Directions:

1. Blend everything together until smooth.

BERRY & CAULIFLOWER SMOOTHIE

Serves: 2
Time: 10 Minutes
Calories: 149
Protein: 3 Grams
Fat: 3 Grams
Carbs: 29 Grams

Ingredients:

- 1 Cup Riced Cauliflower, Frozen
- 1 Cup Banana, Sliced & Frozen
- ½ Cup Mixed Berries, Frozen
- 2 Cups Almond Milk, Unsweetened
- 2 Teaspoons Maple syrup, Pure & Optional

Directions:

1. Blend until mixed well.

GREEN MANGO SMOOTHIE

Serves: 1
Time: 5 Minutes
Calories: 417
Protein: 7.2 Grams
Fat: 2.8 Grams
Carbs: 102.8 Grams

Ingredients:

- 2 Cups Spinach
- 1-2 Cups Coconut Water
- 2 Mangos, Ripe, Peeled & Diced

Directions:

1. Blend everything together until smooth.

FRUIT SALAD

Serves: 4
Time: 15 Minutes
Calories: 276
Protein: 3.1 Grams
Fat: 12.3 Grams
Carbs: 39.7 Grams

Ingredients:

- 1/8 Teaspoon Cinnamon
- 1/8 Teaspoon Cardamom
- 1/8 Teaspoon Ginger
- 1 Tablespoon Dark Brown Sugar (Vegan & Optional)
- 2 Cups Pineapple, Fresh & Cubed
- 1 Cup Banana, Sliced
- 1 Cup Orange Sections
- 1 Cup Mango, Ripe, Diced & Peeled
- 1 Tablespoon Lime, Zest & Juiced

Directions:

1. Toss everything together, and allow it to sit chilling for an hour before serving.

FLAXSEED PORRIDGE

Serves: 2
Time: 15 Minutes
Calories: 405
Protein: 10 Grams
Fat: 34 Grams
Carbs: 12 Grams

Ingredients:

- 1 Cup Almond Milk
- 1 Teaspoon Cinnamon
- ¼ Cup Coconut Flour
- ¼ Cup Ground Flaxseed
- 10 Drops Stevia
- 1 Teaspoon Vanilla Extract, Pure
- Pinch Sea Salt
- 1 Ounces Coconut, Shaved for Garnish
- 2 Ounces Blueberries for Garnish
- 2 Tablespoons Almond Butter for Garnish
- 2 Tablespoons Pumpkin Seeds for Garnish

Directions:

1. Heat your almond milk in a saucepan using low heat, and whisk your coconut flour, salt, cinnamon and flaxseed together.
2. Add in your stevia and vanilla once it's bubbling
3. Remove it from heat, mixing all of your ingredients together.
4. Garnish with blueberries, coconut, pumpkin seeds and almonds before serving.

SPICY HASH BROWNS

Serves: 5
Time: 45 Minutes
Calories: 227
Protein: 3.9 Grams
Fat: 5.7 Grams
Carbs: 41.3 Grams

Ingredients:

- 1 Teaspoon Paprika
- ¼ Teaspoon Red Pepper
- ¾ Teaspoon Chili Powder
- 2 Tablespoons Olive Oil
- 6 ½ Cups Potatoes, Diced
- Sea Salt & Black Pepper to Taste

Directions:

1. Start by heating you oven to 400, and then get out a large bowl.
2. Mix together your olive oil, chili powder, red peppers, salt, black pepper, and paprika. Stir well.
3. Coat your potatoes in the mixture, and then arrange your potatoes on a baking sheet in a single layer
4. Bake for about thirty minutes.

KIWI SLUSHIE

Serves: 2
Time: 5 Minutes
Calories: 42.1
Protein: 0.8 Grams
Fat: 0.4 Grams
Carbs: 10.1 Grams

Ingredients:

- 18 Chocolate Tea Ice Cubes
- 1 Cup Vanilla Rice Milk
- 2 Ripe Kiwi Fruits, Sliced & Frozen

Directions:

1. Blend everything together until smooth.

CHIA SEED SMOOTHIE

Serves: 3
Time: 5 Minutes
Calories: 477
Protein: 8 Grams
Fat: 29 Grams
Carbs: 57 Grams

Ingredients:

- ¼ Teaspoon Cinnamon
- 1 Tablespoon Ginger, Fresh & Grated
- Pinch Cardamom
- 1 Tablespoon Chia Seeds
- 2 Medjool Dates, Pitted
- 1 Cup Alfalfa Sprouts
- 1 Cup Water
- 1 Banana
- ½ Cup Coconut Milk, Unsweetened

Directions:

1. Blend everything together until smooth.

MANGO SMOOTHIE

Serves: 3
Time: 5 Minutes
Calories: 376
Protein: 5 Grams
Fat: 2 Grams
Carbs: 95 Grams

Ingredients:

- 1 Carrot, Peeled & Chopped
- 1 Cup Strawberries
- 1 Cup Water
- 1 Cup Peaches, Chopped
- 1 Banana, Frozen & sliced
- 1 Cup Mango, Chopped

Directions:

1. Blend everything together until smooth.

QUINOA & CHOCOLATE BOWL

Serves: 2
Time: 35 Minutes
Calories: 392
Protein: 12 Grams
Fat: 19 Grams
Carbs: 49 Grams

Ingredients:

- 1 Cup Quinoa
- 1 Cup Almond Milk, Unsweetened
- 1 Teaspoon Cinnamon
- 1 Banana
- 1 Cup Water
- 2-3 Tablespoons Cocoa Powder, Unsweetened
- 2 Tablespoons Almond Butter
- 1 Tablespoon Chia Seeds, Ground
- 2 Tablespoons Walnuts, Optional
- ¼ Cup Raspberries, Fresh

Directions:

1. Place your cinnamon, milk, water and quinoa in a pot, bringing it to a boil before turning it down to low heat to simmer. Cover, simmering for twenty-five to thirty minutes.
2. Puree your banana, mixing in your almond butter, flaxseed and cocoa powder.

3. Scoop a cup of quinoa into a bowl, and then top with pudding, raspberries and walnuts if you're using them before serving.

VEGETABLE HASH

Serves: 4
Time: 35 Minutes
Calories: 273
Protein: 9 Grams
Fat: 11 Grams
Carbs: 39 Grams

Ingredients:

- 1 Tablespoon Sage Leaves, Chopped
- 1 Bell Pepper, Diced
- 3 Cloves Garlic, Minced
- 1 Onion, Diced
- 3 Tablespoons Olive Oil
- 3 Red Potatoes, Diced
- 15 Ounces Black Beans, Canned
- 1 Tablespoon Parsley, Chopped
- 2 Cups Swiss Chard, Chopped
- Sea Salt & Black Pepper to Taste

Directions:

1. Start by cooking your potato, garlic and onion in a skillet with your oil. This will take twenty minutes.
2. Add in your Swiss chard and beans, cooking for three more minutes.
3. Season with salt and pepper, and serve with parsley.

WALNUT PORRIDGE

Serves: 2
Time: 25 Minutes
Calories: 312
Protein: 7 Grams
Fat: 18 Grams
Carbs: 35 Grams

Ingredients:

- 1 ½ Cups Water
- ½ Cup Coconut Milk, Unsweetened
- 1 Cup Teff, Whole Grain
- ½ Teaspoon Cardamom, Ground
- 1 Teaspoon Sea Salt, Fine
- ¼ Cup Walnuts, Chopped
- 1 Tablespoon Maple Syrup, Pure

Directions:

1. Start by combining your coconut oil and water, bringing it to a boil before stirring in your teff.
2. Add the cardamom, and then allow it to simmer for twenty minutes.
3. Mix in your walnuts and maple syrup before serving.

GRANOLA

Serves: 7
Time: 1 Hour 30 Minutes
Calories: 239
Protein: 6 Grams
Fat: 11 Grams
Carbs: 32 Grams

Ingredients:

- ½ Cup Maple Syrup, Pure
- ¼ Cup Coconut Oil
- ¾ Cup Coconut, Unsweetened & Shredded
- 1 Cup Almonds, Slivered
- ¾ Teaspoon Sea Salt, Fine
- 5 Cups Rolled Oats

Directions:

1. Start by heating your oven to 250, and then mix all of your ingredients together in a bowl.
2. Spread your granola out over two baking sheets, making sure it's spread out evenly.
3. Bake for an hour and fifteen minutes, but you'll need to stir every twenty minutes.
4. Allow it to cool before serving.

BREAKFAST CEREAL

Serves: 6
Time: 45 Minutes
Calories: 160
Protein: 3 Grams
Fat: 1.5 Grams
Carbs: 34 Grams

Ingredients:

- ¼ Tablespoon Butter
- 2 ¼ Cups Water
- Honey to Taste
- 1 Teaspoon Cinnamon
- 1 Cup Brown Rice, Uncooked
- ½ Cup Raisins, Seedless

Directions:

1. Start by combining your cinnamon, raisins, rice, and butter in a saucepan before adding in your water. Bring it to a boil, and allow it to simmer while covered for forty minutes. Fluff with a fork.
2. Serve with honey.

FRUITY OATMEAL

Serves: 2
Time: 25 Minutes
Calories: 230
Protein: 4.6 Grams
Fat: 5.6 Grams
Carbs: 43.8 Grams

Ingredients:

- ½ Cup Apple Juice, Fresh & Frozen
- ½ Cup Oatmeal
- ½ Cup Water
- 3 Prunes, Diced
- 1 Apple, Small & Diced
- 4 Pecans, Diced
- 3 Apricots, Dehydrated, Dried & Diced
- ¼ Teaspoon Cinnamon

Directions:

1. Start by getting out a small saucepan and mix together your apple juice and water, bringing the mixture to a boil.
2. Add a half a cup of oatmeal, cooking for a minute. Add in your pecans, cinnamon and fruit pieces. Make sure to stir. If you want to make sure you have more vitamins, add in your fruit when your oatmeal is nearly cool.

LUNCH RECIPES

This chapter will concentrate on lunches that are easy to make while still being delicious. Soups and salads are great on the go!

AVOCADO & RADISH SALAD

Serves: 2
Time: 10 Minutes
Calories: 223
Protein: 3 Grams
Fat: 19 Grams
Carbs: 10 Grams

Ingredients:

- 1 Avocado, Sliced
- 6 Radishes, Sliced
- 2 Tomatoes, Sliced
- 1 Lettuce Head, Leaves Separated
- ½ Red Onion, Peeled & Sliced

Dressing:

- ½ Cup Olive Oil
- ¼ Cup Lime Juice, Fresh
- ¼ Cup Apple Cider Vinegar
- 3 Cloves Garlic, Chopped Fine
- Sea Salt & Black Pepper to Taste

Directions:

1. Spread your lettuce leaves on a platter, and then layer with your onion, tomatoes, avocado and radishes.
2. Whisk your dressing ingredients together before drizzling it over your salad.

BAKED OKRA & TOMATO

Serves: 6
Time: 1 Hour 15 Minutes
Calories: 55
Protein: 3 Grams
Fat: 0 Grams
Carbs: 12 Grams

Ingredients:

- ½ cup Lime Beans, Frozen
- 4 Tomatoes, Chopped
- 8 Ounces Okra, Fresh, Washed & Stemmed, Sliced into ½ Inch Thick Slices
- 1 Onion, Sliced into Rings
- ½ Sweet Pepper, Seeded & Sliced Thin
- Pinch Crushed Red Pepper
- Sea Salt to taste

Directions:

1. Start by heating the oven to 350, and then cook your lime beans. Drain them, and then get out a two-quarter casserole.
2. Combine everything together, and bake covered with foil for fort-five minutes.
3. Stir, and then uncover. Bake for another thirty minutes, and stir before serving.

WATERCRESS & BLOOD ORANGE SALAD

Serves: 4
Time: 10 Minutes
Calories: 94
Protein: 2 Grams
Fat: 5 Grams
Carbs: 13 Grams

Ingredients:

- 1 Tablespoon Hazelnuts, Toasted & Chopped
- 2 Blood Oranges (or Navel Oranges)
- 3 Cups watercress, Stems Removed
- 1/8 Teaspoon Sea Salt, Fine
- 1 Tablespoon Lemon Juice, Fresh
- 1 Tablespoon Honey, Raw
- 1 Tablespoon Water
- 2 Tablespoons Chives, Fresh

Directions:

1. Whisk your oil, honey, lemon juice, chives, salt and water together. Add in your watercress, tossing until it's coated.
2. Arrange the mixture onto salad plates, and top with orange slices. Drizzle with remaining liquid, and sprinkle with hazelnuts.

LENTIL POTATO SALAD

Serves: 2
Time: 35 Minutes
Calories: 400
Protein: 7 Grams
Fat: 26 Grams
Carbs: 39 Grams

Ingredients:

- ½ Cup Beluga Lentils
- 8 Fingerling Potatoes
- 1 Cup Scallions, Sliced Thin
- ¼ Cup Cherry Tomatoes, Halved
- ¼ Cup Lemon Vinaigrette
- Sea Salt & Black Pepper to Taste

Directions:

1. Bring two cups of water to simmer in a pot, adding your lentils. Cook for twenty to twenty-five minutes, and then drain. Your lentils should be tender.
2. Bring another pot of salted water to a boil, and add in your potatoes. Reduce to a simmer, cooking for fifteen minutes, and then drain. Halve your potatoes once they're cool enough to touch.
3. Put your lentils on a serving plate, and then top with scallions, potatoes and tomatoes. Drizzle with your vinaigrette, and season with salt and pepper.

EDAMAME SALAD

Serves: 1
Time: 15 Minutes
Calories: 299
Protein: 20 Grams
Fat: 9 Grams
Carbs: 38 Grams

Ingredients:

- ¼ Cup Red Onion, Chopped
- 1 Cup Corn Kernels, Fresh
- 1 Cup Edamame Beans, Shelled & Thawed
- 1 Red Bell Pepper, Chopped
- 2-3 Tablespoons Lime Juice, Fresh
- 5-6 Basil Leaves, Fresh & Sliced
- 5-6 Mint Leaves, Fresh & Sliced
- Sea Salt & Black Pepper to Taste

Directions:

1. Place everything into a Mason jar, and then seal the jar tightly. Shake well before serving.

CAULIFLOWER & APPLE SALAD

Serves: 4
Time: 25 Minutes
Calories: 198
Protein: 7 Grams
Fat: 8 Grams
Carbs: 32 Grams

Ingredients:

- 3 Cups Cauliflower, Chopped into Florets
- 2 Cups Baby Kale
- 1 Sweet Apple, Cored & Chopped
- ¼ Cup Basil, Fresh & Chopped
- ¼ Cup Mint, Fresh & Chopped
- ¼ Cup Parsley, Fresh & Chopped
- 1/3 Cup Scallions, Sliced Thin
- 2 Tablespoons Yellow Raisins
- 1 Tablespoon Sun Dried Tomatoes, Chopped
- ½ Cup Miso Dressing, Optional
- ¼ Cup Roasted Pumpkin Seeds, Optional

Directions:

1. Combine everything together, tossing before serving.

OLIVE & FENNEL SALAD

Serves: 3
Time: 5 Minutes
Calories: 331
Protein: 3 Grams
Fat: 29 Grams
Carbs: 15 Grams

Ingredients:

- 6 Tablespoons Olive Oil
- 3 Fennel Bulbs, Trimmed, Cored & Quartered
- 2 Tablespoons Parsley, Fresh & Chopped
- 1 Lemon, Juiced & Zested
- 12 Black Olives
- Sea Salt & Black Pepper to Taste

Directions:

1. Grease your baking dish, and then place your fennel in it. Make sure the cut side is up.
2. Mix your lemon zest, lemon juice, salt, pepper and oil, pouring it over your fennel.
3. Sprinkle your olives over it, and bake at 400.
4. Serve with parsley.

RED PEPPER & BROCCOLI SALAD

Serves: 2
Time: 15 Minutes
Calories: 185
Protein: 4 Grams
Fat: 14 Grams
Carbs: 8 Grams

Ingredients:

- Ounces Lettuce Salad Mix
- 1 Head Broccoli, Chopped into Florets
- 1 Red Pepper, Seeded & Chopped

Dressing:

- 3 Tablespoons White Wine Vinegar
- 1 Teaspoon Dijon Mustard
- 1 Clove Garlic, Peeled & Chopped Fine
- ½ Teaspoon Black Pepper
- ½ Teaspoon Sea Salt, Fine
- 2 Tablespoons Olive Oil
- 1 Tablespoon Parsley, Chopped

Directions:

1. Blanch your broccoli in boiling water, and then drain it. Drain it on a paper towel.
2. Whisk together all dressing ingredients.
3. Toss ingredients together before serving.

ZUCCHINI & LEMON SALAD

Serves: 2
Time: 3 Hours 10 Minutes
Calories: 159
Protein: 3 Grams
Fat: 14 Grams
Net Carbs: 7 Grams

Ingredients:

- 1 Green Zucchini, Sliced into Rounds
- 1 Yellow Squash, Zucchini, Sliced into Rounds
- 1 Clove Garlic, Peeled & Chopped
- 2 Tablespoons Olive Oil
- 2 Tablespoons Basil, Fresh
- 1 Lemon, Juiced & Zested
- ¼ Cup Coconut Milk
- Sea Salt & Black Pepper to Taste

Directions:

1. Toss all of your ingredients in a bowl, refrigerating for three hours before serving.

MEDITERRANEAN WRAP

Serves: 1
Time: 10 Minutes
Calories: 428
Protein: 13 Grams
Fat: 23 Grams
Carbs: 47 Grams

Ingredients:

- ¼ Cup Crispy Chickpeas
- ¼ Cup Cherry Tomatoes, Halved
- Handful Baby Spinach
- 2 Romaine Lettuce Leaves for Wrapping
- 2 Tablespoons Lemon Juice, Fresh
- ¼ Cup Hummus
- 2 Tablespoons Kalamata Olives, Quartered

Directions:

1. Mix everything but your lettuce leaves and hummus together.
2. Put your hummus on your lettuce leaves, topping with your chickpea mixture, and then serve immediately.

QUINOA WITH NECTARINE SLAW

Serves: 2
Time: 20 Minutes
Calories: 396
Protein: 11 Grams
Fat: 18 Grams
Carbs: 52 Grams

Ingredients:

- ½ Cup Kale, Chopped
- 1/3 Cup Pumpkin Seeds, Roasted
- 3 Tablespoons Lemon Vinaigrette
- 1 Teaspoon Nutritional Yeast (Optional)
- 1/3 Cup Scallions, Sliced Thin
- 1 Cup Quinoa, Cooked & Room Temperature
- 2 Nectarines, Chopped into ½ Inch Wedges
- ½ Cup White Cabbage, Shredded

Directions:

1. Combine everything together in a bowl before serving.

SUMMER CHICKPEA SALAD

Serves: 4
Time: 15 Minutes
Calories: 145
Protein: 4 Grams
Fat: 7.5 Grams
Carbs: 16 Grams

Ingredients:

- 1 ½ Cups Cherry Tomatoes, Halved
- 1 Cup English Cucumber, Slices
- 1 Cup Chickpeas, Canned, Unsalted, Drained & Rinsed
- 1/3 Cup Flat Leaf Parsley, Roughly Chopped
- ¼ Cup Red Onion, Slivered
- 2 Tablespoon Olive Oil
- 1 ½ Tablespoons Lemon Juice, Fresh
- 1 ½ Tablespoons Lemon Juice, Fresh
- Sea Salt & Black Pepper to Taste

Directions:

1. Mix everything together, and toss to combine before serving.

CORN & BLACK BEAN SALAD

Salad: 6
Time: 10 Minutes
Calories: 159
Protein: 6.4 Grams
Fat: 5.6 Grams
Carbs: 23.7 Grams

Ingredients:

- ¼ Cup Cilantro, Fresh & Chopped
- 1 Can Corn, Drained (10 Ounces)
- 1/8 Cup Red Onion, Chopped
- 1 Can Black Beans, Drained (15 Ounces)
- 1 Tomato, Chopped
- 3 Tablespoons Lemon Juice, Fresh
- 2 Tablespoons Olive Oil
- Sea Salt & Black Pepper to Taste

Directions:

1. Mix everything together, and then refrigerate until cool. Serve cold.

PARSLEY SALAD

Serves: 8
Time: 30 Minutes
Calories: 165.2
Protein: 3.8 Grams
Fat: 9.1 Grams
Carbs: 20.1 Grams

Ingredients:

- 3 Lemons, Juiced
- 150 Grams Flat Lea Parsley, Chopped Fine
- 1 Cup Boiled Water
- 5 Tablespoons Olive Oil
- Sea Salt & Black Pepper to Taste
- 6 Green Onions, Chopped Fine
- 1 Cup Bulgur
- 4 Tomatoes, Chopped Fine

Directions:

1. Add your Bulgur to your water, and mix well. Put a towel on top of it to steam it. Keep it to the side, and then chop your spring onions, tomatoes and parsley. Put them in your salad bowl.
2. Pour your juice into the mixture, and then add in your olive oil, salt and pepper.
3. Put this mixture over your bulgur to serve.

RED LENTIL SOUP

Serves: 4
Time: 50 Minutes
Calories: 188
Protein: 12.5 Grams
Fat: 1.2 Grams
Carbs: 33.6 Grams

Ingredients:

- 1 Teaspoon Paprika
- 4 Cups Vegetable Stock
- ¼ Cup Onion, Chopped Fine
- 1 Cup Lentil, Red, Washed & Cleaned
- ½ Cup Potato, Peeled & Diced
- Sea Salt & Black Pepper to Taste

Directions:

1. Rinse your lentils under cold water, and then get out a medium pot.
2. Place your red lentils, potatoes, stock, onion and paprika in the pot.
3. Bring it to a boil, and then decrease the heat to allow it to simmer.
4. Put the lid on loosely, and cook until your lentils are tender. This will take roughly thirty minutes.
5. Add your salt and pepper, put a cup of the soup in the food processor, and then place the blended soup back into the pot.
6. Serve warm.

MAC & "CHEESE"

Serves: 6
Time: 40 Minutes
Calories: 848
Protein: 70 Grams
Fat: 8.4 Grams
Carbs: 140.1 Grams

Ingredients:

- Milk Substitute
- 16 Ounces Elbow Macaroni, Whole Wheat
- 16 Ounces Vegan Mayonnaise
- 3 Cups Nutritional Yeast
- Whole Wheat Bread Crumbs
- Sea Salt & Black Pepper to Taste

Directions:

1. Start by heating your oven to 350, and then make your noodles as the package instructs. Drain them, and then add in your ingredients, and mix well.
2. Add in your milk substitute, stirring until creamy.
3. Pour your ingredients into a baking dish and then sprinkle your bread crumbs on top.
4. Bake until it's golden brown, which will take about a half hour.

THAI SQUASH SOUP

Serves: 2
Time: 30 Minutes
Calories: 717.3
Protein: 10.3 Grams
Fat: 48.3 Grams
Carbs: 77.4 Grams

Ingredients:

- 1 Teaspoon Curry Powder
- 1 Tablespoon Olive Oil
- 1 Red Onion, Chopped
- 1 Pint Vegetable Stock
- 1 Butter Squash, Chunked
- 1 Can Coconut Milk (Roughly 13.5 Ounces)

Directions:

1. Get out a pan and heat your olive oil. Once it's heated, add in your onion and cook to soften. This should take two to three minutes. Add your butternut squash, stock to taste, and curry powder.
2. Bring it to a boil, and then reduce to simmer. The squash should become tender.
3. Stir in your coconut milk, and then blend until smooth.
4. Return it to the pan to warm, and season with salt and pepper before serving.

BUTTER BEAN HUMMUS

Serves: 4
Time: 5 Minutes
Calories: 150
Protein: 8 Grams
Fat: 4 Grams
Carbs: 23 Grams

Ingredients:

- 1 Can Butter Beans, Drained & Rinsed
- 4 Sprigs Parsley, Minced
- 1 Tablespoon Olive Oil
- ½ Lemon, Juiced
- 2 Cloves Garlic, Minced
- Sea Salt to Taste

Directions:

1. Blend all of your ingredients together, and then serve as a dip with fresh vegetables.

SPINACH & ORANGE SALAD

Serves: 6
Time: 15 Minutes
Calories: 99
Protein: 2.5 Grams
Fat: 5 Grams
Carbs: 13.1 Grams

Ingredients:

- ¼ -1/3 Cup Vegan Dressing
- 3 Oranges, Medium, Peeled, Seeded & Sectioned
- ¾ lb. Spinach, Fresh & Torn
- 1 Red Onion, Medium, Sliced & Separated into Rings

Directions:

1. Toss everything together, and serve with dressing.

LENTIL & SWEET POTATO SOUP

Serves: 6
Time: 40 Minutes
Calories: 323
Protein: 16 Grams
Fat: 3.4 Grams
Carbs: 58.5 Grams

Ingredients:

- 1 Cup Red Lentil
- 750 Grams Sweet Potatoes
- ¼ Teaspoon Cayenne
- 3 Onions
- 1 lemon
- 5 Cloves Garlic
- ½ Teaspoon Turmeric
- ½ Cup Coriander, Chopped
- 5 Cups Water
- 2 Teaspoon Cumin
- Sea Salt & Black Pepper to Taste

Directions:

1. Start by peeling and chopping your onion and sweet potatoes, and it can be a little thick.
2. Combine your garlic, water, lentils, cumin, turmeric and cumin together in a pot.
3. Bring it to a boil, and allow it to simmer for a half hour.
4. Puree your soup before adding in your lemon juice and coriander. Season with salt and pepper to taste.

FRUITY KALE SALAD

Serves: 4
Time: 30 Minutes
Calories: 220
Protein: 4 Grams
Fat: 17 Grams
Carbs: 16 Grams

Ingredients:

Salad:

- 10 Ounces Baby Kale
- ½ Cup Pomegranate Arils
- 1 Tablespoon Olive Oil
- 1 Apple, Sliced

Dressing:

- 3 Tablespoons Apple Cider Vinegar
- 3 Tablespoons Olive Oil
- 1 Tablespoon Tahini Sauce (Optional)
- Sea Salt & Black Pepper to Taste

Directions:

1. Wash and dry the kale. If kale is too expensive, you can also use lettuce, arugula or spinach. Take the stems out, and chop it.
2. Combine all of your salad ingredients together.
3. Combine all of your dressing ingredients together before drizzling it over the salad to serve.

BLACK EYED PEAS STEW

Serves: 5
Time: 30 Minutes
Calories: 338
Protein: 21 Grams
Fat: 4 Grams
Carbs: 58 Grams

Ingredients:

- 1 Can Tomatoes, Crushed
- ¼ Teaspoon Cayenne
- 1 Clove Garlic
- 2 Tablespoons Olive Oil
- 1 Onion
- 2 Cans Black Eyed Peas, Drained
- 8 Ounces Okra, Frozen & Thawed
- Sea Salt to Taste

Directions:

1. Start by brown your onion using olive oil, and then add in your garlic and cayenne. Cook for another minute.
2. Mix in all of your remaining ingredients, simmering until your okra becomes soft.

WHITE BEAN & SPINACH SOUP

Serves: 4
Time: 25 Minutes
Calories: 218
Protein: 12 Grams
Fat: 3.3 Grams
Carbs: 37.9 Grams

Ingredients:

- 3 Cups Baby Spinach, Cleaned & Trimmed
- 1 Can White Beans (Roughly 14.5 Ounces)
- 3-4 Cups Vegetable Stock, Homemade
- 1 Shallot, Diced Fine
- 1 Clove Garlic, Minced Fine
- 14.5 Ounces Tomatoes, Diced
- 1 Teaspoon Rosemary
- ½ Cup Shell Pasta, Whole Wheat
- 2 Teaspoons Olive Oil
- Red Pepper Flakes to Taste
- Black Pepper to Taste

Directions:

1. Start by heating your olive oil in a saucepan before sautéing your garlic and shallots
2. Add in your rosemary, beans, broth and tomatoes. Season with your red pepper flakes and black pepper.
3. Put your pasta in, cooking for ten minutes, and then add in your spinach. Cook until it's wilted.

DINNER RECIPES

Here are some easy dinner recipes that won't break the bank and will delight the taste buds.

TOFU & ASPARAGUS STIR FRY

Serves: 3
Time: 20 Minutes
Calories: 380
Protein: 22 Grams
Fat: 24 Grams
Carbs: 27 Grams

Ingredients:

- 1 Tablespoon Ginger, Peeled & Grated
- 8 Ounces Firm Tofu, Chopped into Slices
- 4 Green Onions, Sliced Thin
- Toasted Sesame Oil to Taste
- 1 Bunch Asparagus, Trimmed & Chopped
- 1 Handful Cashew Nuts, Chopped & Toasted
- 2 Tablespoons Hoisin Sauce
- 1 Lime, Juiced & Zested
- 1 Handful Mint, Fresh & Chopped
- 1 Handful Basil, Fresh & Chopped
- 3 Cloves Garlic, Chopped

- 3 Handfuls Spinach, Chopped
- Pinch Sea Salt

Directions:

1. Get out a wok and heat up your oil. Add in your tofu, cooking for a few minutes.
2. Put your tofu to the side, and then sauté your red pepper flakes, ginger, salt, onions and asparagus for a minute.
3. Mix in your spinach, garlic, and cashews, cooking for another two minutes.
4. Add your tofu back in, and then drizzle in your lime juice, lime zest, hoisin sauce, cooking for another half a minute.
5. Remove it from heat, adding in your mint and basil.

CAULIFLOWER STEAKS

Serves: 4
Time: 30 Minutes
Calories: 167
Protein: 6 Grams
Fat: 13 Grams
Carbs: 10 Grams

Ingredients:

- ¼ Teaspoon Black Pepper
- ½ Teaspoon Sea Salt, Fine
- 1 Tablespoon Olive Oil
- 1 Head Cauliflower, Large
- ¼ Cup Creamy Hummus
- 2 Tablespoons Lemon Sauce
- ½ Cup Peanuts, Crushed (Optional)

Directions:

1. Start by heating your oven to 425.
2. Cut your cauliflower stems, and then remove the leaves. Put the cut side down, and then slice half down the middle. Cut into ¾ inch steaks. If you cut them thinner, they could fall apart.
3. Arrange them in a single layer on a baking sheet, drizzling with oil. Season with salt and pepper, and bake for twenty to twenty-five minutes. They should be lightly browned and tender.

4. Spread your hummus on the steaks, drizzling with your lemon sauce. Top with peanuts if you're using it.

TOFU POKE

Serves: 4
Time: 30 Minutes
Calories: 262
Protein: 16 Grams
Fat: 15 Grams
Carbs: 19 Grams

Ingredients:

- ¾ Cup Scallions, Sliced Thin
- 1 ½ Tablespoons Mirin
- ¼ Cup Tamari
- 1 ½ Tablespoon Dark Sesame Oil, Toasted
- 1 Tablespoon Sesame Seeds, Toasted (Optional)
- 2 Teaspoons Ginger, fresh & Grated
- ½ Teaspoon Red Pepper, crushed
- 12 Ounces Extra Firm Tofu, Drained & Cut into ½ Inch Pieces
- 4 Cups Zucchini Noodles
- 2 Tablespoons Rice Vinegar
- 2 Cups Carrots, Shredded
- 2 Cups Pea Shoots
- ¼ Cup Basil, Fresh & Chopped
- ¼ Cup Peanuts, Toasted & Chopped (Optional)

Directions:

1. Wisk your tamari, mirin, sesame seeds, oil, ginger, red pepper, and scallion greens in a bowl. Set two tablespoons of this sauce aside, and add the tofu to the remaining sauce. Toss to coat.
2. Combine your vinegar and zucchini noodles in a bowl.
3. Divide it between four bowls, topping with tofu, carrots, and a tablespoon of basil and peanuts.
4. Drizzle with sauce before serving.

RATATOUILLE

Serves: 10
Time: 1 Hour 15 Minutes
Calories: 90
Protein: 3 Grams
Fat: 25 Grams
Carbs: 13 Grams

Ingredients:

- 2 Tablespoons Olive Oil
- 2 Eggplants, Peeled & Cubed
- 8 Zucchini, Chopped
- 4 Tomatoes, Chopped
- ¼ Cup Basil, Chopped
- 4 Thyme Sprigs
- 2 Yellow Onions, Diced
- 3 Cloves Garlic, Minced
- 3 Bell Peppers, Chopped
- 1 Bay Leaf
- Sea Salt to Taste

Directions:

1. Salt your eggplant and leave it in a strainer.
2. Heat a teaspoon of oil in a Dutch oven, cooking your onions for ten minutes. Season with salt.

3. Mix your peppers in, cooking for five more minutes.
4. Place this mixture in a bowl.
5. Heat your oil and sauté zucchini, sprinkling with salt. Cook for five minutes, and place it in the same bowl.
6. Rinse your eggplant, squeezing the water out, and heat another two teaspoons of oil in your Dutch oven. Cook your eggplant for ten minutes, placing it in your vegetable bowl.
7. Heat the remaining oil and cook your garlic. Add in your tomatoes, thyme sprigs and bay leaves to deglaze the bottom.
8. Toss your vegetables back in, and then bring it to a simmer.
9. Simmer for forty-five minutes, and make sure to stir. Discard your thyme and bay leaf. Mix in your basil and serve warm.

TOMATO GAZPACHO

Serves: 6
Time: 2 Hours 25 Minutes
Calories: 181
Protein: 3 Grams
Fat: 14 Grams
Carbs: 14 Grams

Ingredients:

- 2 Tablespoons + 1 Teaspoon Red Wine Vinegar, Divided
- ½ Teaspoon Pepper
- 1 Teaspoon Sea Salt
- 1 Avocado,
- ¼ Cup Basil, Fresh & Chopped
- 3 Tablespoons + 2 Teaspoons Olive Oil, Divided
- 1 Clove Garlic, crushed
- 1 Red Bell Pepper, Sliced & Seeded
- 1 Cucumber, Chunked
- 2 ½ lbs. Large Tomatoes, Cored & Chopped

Directions:

1. Place half of your cucumber, bell pepper, and ¼ cup of each tomatoes in a bowl, covering. Set it in the fried.
2. Puree your remaining tomatoes, cucumber and bell pepper with garlic, three tablespoons oil, two tablespoons of vinegar, sea salt and black pepper into a blender, blending until smooth. Transfer it to a bowl, and chill for two hours.
3. Chop the avocado, adding it to your chopped vegetables, adding your remaining oil, vinegar, salt, pepper and basil.
4. Ladle your tomato puree mixture into bowls, and serve with chopped vegetables as a salad.

SIMPLE CHILI

Serves: 4
Time: 30 Minutes
Calories: 160
Protein: 8 Grams
Fat: 3 Grams
Carbs: 29 Grams

Ingredients:

- 1 Onion, Diced
- 1 Teaspoon Olive Oil
- 3 Cloves Garlic, Minced
- 28 Ounces Tomatoes, Canned
- ¼ Cup Tomato Paste
- 14 Ounces Kidney Beans, Canned, Rinsed & Dried
- 2-3 Teaspoons Chili Powder
- ¼ Cup Cilantro, Fresh (or Parsley)
- ¼ Teaspoon Sea Salt, Fine

Directions:

1. Get out a pot, and sauté your onion and garlic in your oil at the bottom cook for five minutes. Add in your tomato paste, tomatoes, beans, and chili powder. Season with salt.
2. Allow it to simmer for ten to twenty minutes.
3. Garnish with cilantro or parsley to serve.

CAULIFLOWER RICE TABBOULEH

Serves: 4
Time: 20 Minutes
Calories: 220
Protein: 7 Grams
Fat: 15 Grams
Carbs: 20 Grams

Ingredients:

- 4 Cups Cauliflower Rice
- 1 ½ Cups Cherry Tomatoes, Quartered
- 3-4 Tablespoons Olive Oil
- 1 Cup Parsley, Fresh & Chopped
- 1 Cup Mint, Fresh & Chopped
- 1 Cup Snap Peas, Sliced Thin
- 1 Small Cucumber, Cut into ¼ Inch Pieces
- ¼ Cup Scallions, Sliced Thin
- 3-4 Tablespoons Lemon Juice, Fresh
- 1 Teaspoon Sea Salt, Fine
- ½ Teaspoon Black Pepper

Directions:

1. Get out a bowl and combine your cauliflower rice, tomatoes, mint, parsley, cucumbers, scallions and snap peas together. Toss until combined.
2. Add your olive oil and lemon juice before tossing again. Season with salt and pepper.

DIJON MAPLE BURGERS

Serves: 12
Time: 50 Minutes
Calories: 200
Protein: 8 Grams
Fat: 11 Grams
Carbs: 21 Grams

Ingredients:

- 1 Red Bell Pepper
- 19 Ounces Can Chickpeas, Rinsed & Drained
- 1 Cup Almonds, Ground
- 2 Teaspoons Dijon Mustard
- 1 Teaspoon Oregano
- ½ Teaspoon Sage
- 1 Cup Spinach, Fresh
- 1 – ½ Cups Rolled Oats
- 1 Clove Garlic, Pressed
- ½ Lemon, Juiced
- 2 Teaspoons Maple Syrup, Pure

Directions:

1. Start by heating your oven to 350, and then get out a baking sheet. Line it with parchment paper.
2. Cut your red pepper in half and then take the seeds out. Place it on your baking sheet, and roast in the oven while you prepare your other ingredients.
3. Process your chickpeas, almonds, mustard and maple syrup together in a food processor.
4. Add in your lemon juice, oregano, sage, garlic and spinach, processing again. Make sure it's combined, but don't puree it.
5. Once your red bell pepper is softened, which should roughly take ten minutes, add this to the processor as well. Add in your oats, mixing well.
6. Form twelve patties, cooking in the oven for a half hour. They should be browned.

SUSHI BOWL

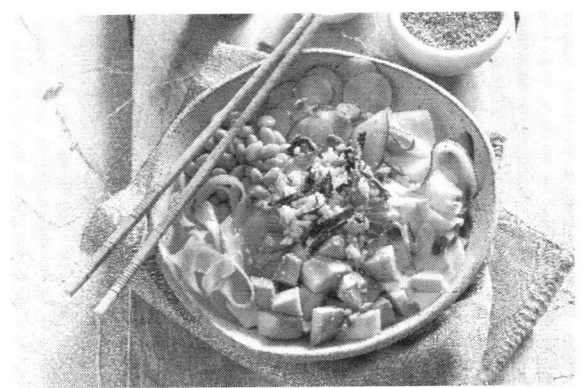

Serves: 1
Time: 40 Minutes
Calories: 467
Protein: 22 Grams
Fat: 20 Grams
Carbs: 56 Grams

Ingredients:

- ½ Cup Edamame Beans, Shelled & Fresh
- ¾ Cup Brown Rice, Cooked
- ½ Cup Spinach, Chopped
- ¼ Cup Bell Pepper, Sliced
- ¼ Cup Avocado, Sliced
- ¼ Cup Cilantro, Fresh & Chopped
- 1 Scallion, Chopped
- ¼ Nori Sheet
- 1-2 Tablespoons Tamari
- 1 Tablespoon Sesame Seeds, Optional

Directions:

1. Steam your edamame beans, and then assemble your edamame, rice, avocado, spinach, cilantro, scallions and bell pepper into a bowl.
2. Cut the nori into ribbons, sprinkling it on top, drizzling with tamari and sesame seeds before serving.

PESTO & TOMATO QUINOA

Serves: 1
Time: 25 Minutes
Calories: 535
Protein: 20 Grams
Fat: 23 Grams
Carbs: 69 Grams

Ingredients:

- 1 Teaspoon Olive Oil
- 1 Cup Onion, Chopped
- 1 Cup Zucchini, Chopped
- 1 Clove Garlic, Minced
- 1 Tomato, Chopped
- Pinch Sea Salt
- 2 Tablespoons Sun Dried Tomatoes, Chopped
- 2-3 Tablespoons Basil Pesto
- 1 Cup Spinach, Chopped
- 2 Cups Quinoa, Cooked
- 1 Tablespoon Nutritional Yeast, Optional

Directions:

1. Heat your oil in a skillet, and sauté your onion over medium-high heat. This should take five minutes, and then add in your garlic, cooking for another minute. Add in your sea salt and zucchini.
2. Cook for about five-minute and then add in your sun dried tomatoes, and mix well.
3. Toss your pesto in, and then mix well.
4. Layer your spinach, quinoa and then zucchini mixture on a plate, topping with nutritional yeast if desired.

SESAME BOK CHOY

Serves: 4
Time: 13 Minutes
Calories: 76
Protein: 4.4 Grams
Fat: 2.7 Grams
Carbs: 9.8 Grams

Ingredients:

- 1 Head Bok Choy
- 1 Teaspoon Canola Oil
- 1/3 Cup Green Onion, Chopped
- 1 Tablespoon Brown Sugar
- 1 ½ Tablespoon Soy Sauce, Light
- 1 Tablespoon Rice Wine
- ½ Teaspoon Ginger, Ground
- 1 Tablespoon Sesame Seeds

Directions:

1. Cut the stems and tops of your bok choy into one inch pieces.
2. Mix together all remaining ingredients in a bowl.
3. Add your bok choy, and top with your dressing.
4. Fry until tender, which should take eight to ten minutes.

STUFFED BELL PEPPER

Serves: 4
Time: 25 Minutes
Calories: 126
Protein: 3 Grams
Fat: 5 Grams
Carbs: 19 Grams

Ingredients:

- 4 Bell Peppers, Halved & Hollowed
- ½ Cup Quinoa, Cooked
- 12 Black Olives, Halved
- 1/3 Cup Tomatoes, Sun Dried
- ½ Cup Baby Spinach
- 2 Cloves Garlic, Minced
- Sea Salt & Black Pepper to Taste

Directions:

1. Bake your peppers at 400 for ten minutes, and then mix the rest of your ingredients in a bowl.
2. Stuff your peppers with the quinoa mixture.

CABBAGE & BEET STEW

Serves: 4
Time: 30 Minutes
Calories: 95
Protein: 1 Gram
Fat: 7 Grams
Carbs: 10 Grams

Ingredients:

- 2 Tablespoons Olive Oil
- 3 Cups Vegetable Broth
- 2 Tablespoons Lemon Juice, Fresh
- ½ Teaspoon Garlic Powder
- ½ Cup Carrots, Shredded
- 2 Cups Cabbage, Shredded
- 1 Cup Beets, Shredded
- Dill for Garnish
- ½ Teaspoon Onion Powder
- Sea Salt & Black Pepper to Taste

Directions:

1. Start by heating up your oil in a pot, and then sauté your vegetables.
2. Pour your broth in, mixing in your seasoning. Simmer until it's cooked through, and then top with dill.

BLACK BEAN BURGERS

Serves: 6
Time: 25 Minutes
Calories: 173
Protein: 7.3 Grams
Fat: 3.2 Grams
Carbs: 29.7 Grams

Ingredients:

- 1 Onion, Diced
- ½ Cup Corn Nibs
- 2 Cloves Garlic, Minced
- ½ Teaspoon Oregano, Dried
- ½ Cup Flour
- 1 Jalapeno Pepper, Small
- 2 Cups Black Beans, Mashed & Canned
- ¼ Cup Breadcrumbs (Vegan)
- 2 Teaspoons Parsley, Minced
- ¼ Teaspoon Cumin
- 1 Tablespoon Olive Oil
- 2 Teaspoons Chili Powder
- ½ Red Pepper, Diced
- Sea Salt to Taste

Directions:

1. Set your flour on a plate, and then get out your garlic, onion, peppers and oregano, throwing it in a pan. Cook over medium-high heat, and then cook until the onions are translucent. Place the peppers in, and sauté until tender.
2. Cook for two minutes, and then set it to the side.
3. Use a potato masher to mash your black beans, and then stir in the vegetables, cumin, breadcrumbs, parsley, salt and chili powder, and then divide it into six patties.
4. Coat each side, and then cook until it's fried on each side. It should take ten minutes. It should be cooked all the way through.

GRILLED EGGPLANT STEAKS

Serves: 6
Time: 35 Minutes
Calories: 86
Protein: 8 Grams
Fat: 7 Grams
Carbs: 12 Grams

Ingredients:

- 4 Roma Tomatoes, Diced
- 8 Ounces Feta, Diced
- 2 Eggplants
- 1 Tablespoon Olive Oil
- 1 Cup Parsley, Chopped
- 1 Cucumber, Diced
- Sea Salt & Black Pepper to Taste

Directions:

1. Slice your eggplants into three thick steaks, and then drizzle with oil. Season it with salt and pepper, and then grill for four minutes per side in a pan.
2. Top with the remaining ingredients.

VEGETABLE STIR FRY

Serves: 10
Time: 25 Minutes
Calories: 50
Protein: 2 Grams
Fat: 2 Grams
Carbs: 6 Grams

Ingredients:

- 1 Tablespoon Oil
- 1 Onion, Sliced
- 1 Cup Carrots, Sliced
- 2 Cups Sugar Snap Peas
- 2 Cups Broccoli Florets
- 1 Bell Pepper, Cut into Strips
- 1 Tablespoon Soy Sauce
- 1 Teaspoon Garlic, Minced

Directions:

1. Combine your carrots and onion into your wok, adding in your oil. Stir fry for two minutes, and then add in the rest of your vegetables.
2. Stir for another seven minutes, and then add in your garlic and soy sauce. Stir fry until blended and hot.

FRIED PINEAPPLE RICE

Serves: 6
Time: 30 Minutes
Calories: 179
Protein: 3 Grams
Fat: 4.4 Grams
Carbs: 32.6 Grams

Ingredients:

- 2-3 Cups Brown Rice, Cooked & Cooled
- 1 Tablespoon Sesame Oil
- 2 Tablespoons Raisins (Optional)
- 1 Onion, Small & Chopped
- ½ -3/4 Cup Pineapple, Chopped
- 1 Tablespoon Soy Sauce (Or Braggs Liquid Amino)
- ½ Teaspoon Turmeric
- 1 Tomato, Chopped
- 1 Teaspoon Curry Powder
- 2 Tablespoons Cilantro, Fresh & Chopped
- Sea Salt & Black Pepper to Taste

Directions:

1. Start by getting out a sauce pan, and then add your sesame oil to the pan. Sauté your onions until they turn translucent.
2. Add in your cooked rice, soy sauce, pineapple, curry powder and turmeric.
3. Mix well and cook for eight to ten minutes.
4. Serve with cilantro, and season with salt and pepper.

BONUS RECIPES! DESSERTS & SNACKS

It's hard to stick to a recipe if you can't have a snack or dessert from time to time, which is where this chapter can help.

TOFU SAAG

Serves: 6
Time: 50 Minutes
Calories: 210
Protein: 12 Grams
Fat: 13.7 Grams
Carbs: 13 Grams

Ingredients:

- 21 Ounces Water Packed Tofu, Fir & Cubed into 1 Inch Pieces
- 10 Ounces Baby Spinach, Torn
- 2 Tablespoons Canola Oil, Divided
- 10 Ounces Baby Kale, Stemmed
- 1 Teaspoon Cumin
- 1 Teaspoon Fennel
- 8 Green Cardamom Pods
- 6 Whole Cloves
- 3 Red Chilies, Red
- 2 Tablespoon Ginger, Fresh & Minced

- Sea Salt to Tate
- 1 Teaspoon Water
- 1/8 Teaspoon Red Pepper

Directions:

1. Cook your tofu in two batches, making sure to drain it on paper towels. Your tofu should be golden.
2. Get out a Dutch oven and then bring two inches of water to a boil, adding in your kale and spinach. Cover and cook until wilted. This should take four minutes, and then stir occasionally. Drain well, and reserve the cooking liquid. Place your spinach and kale into a blender, and blend until smooth. Use your cooking liquid as needed to blend.
3. Combine a tablespoon of oil, a teaspoon of cumin seeds, fennel, and red chilies to a skillet. Cook for two minutes until golden brown and fragrant. Make sure to stir frequently.
4. Stir in your ginger, and cook for thirty seconds. Remove your cardamom and cloves, and then discard them.
5. Stir in your spinach, and then add a quarter cup of cooking liquid into a blender, making a puree. Scrape it down, and then put it in the pan. Stir in your salt, and then cook for five more minutes.
6. Put your tofu on top of your spinach mix, and then cover. Cook for another five more minutes.
7. Combine your ghee, cumin, fennel, and remaining red chilies. Cook for two minutes, and then add in your ground red pepper. Add in a teaspoon of water, and then stir to mix before serving.

MANGO STICKY RICE

Serves: 3
Time: 35 Minutes
Calories: 571
Protein: 6 Grams
Fat: 29.6 Grams
Carbs: 77.6 Grams

Ingredients:

- ½ Cup Sugar
- 1 Mango, Sliced
- 14 Ounces Coconut Milk, Canned
- ½ Cup Basmati Rice

Directions:

1. Cook your rice per package instructions, and add half of your sugar. When cooking your rice, substitute half of your water for half of your coconut milk.
2. Boil your remaining coconut milk in a saucepan with your remaining sugar.
3. Boil on high heat until it's thick, and then add in your mango slices.

OATMEAL SPONGE COOKIES

Serves: 12
Time: 25 Minutes
Calories: 79.1
Protein: 2 Grams
Fat: 1 Gram
Carbs: 16.4 Grams

Ingredients:

- ¼ Cup Applesauce
- ½ Teaspoon Cinnamon
- 1/3 Cup Raisins
- ½ Teaspoon Vanilla Extract, Pure
- 1 Cup Ripe Banana, Mashed
- 2 Cups Oatmeal

Directions:

1. Start by heating your oven to 350.
2. Mix everything together. It should be gooey.
3. Drop it onto an ungreased baking sheet by the tablespoon, and then flatten.
4. Bake for fifteen minutes.

KALE CHIPS

Serves: 4
Time: 25 Minutes
Calories: 25.1
Protein: 1.7 Grams
Fat: 0.4 Grams
Carbs: 5 Grams

Ingredients:

- 1 Bunch Kale
- 1 Spritz Olive Oil

Directions:

1. Heat your oven to 250, and then wash your kale before patting it dry.
2. Arrange your kale on a prepared baking sheet, making sure your kale doesn't overlap. Spray it down with olive oil, and then season with salt.
3. Cook for twenty minutes.

ZUCCHINI BROWNIES

Serves: 24
Time: 45 Minutes
Calories: 138
Protein: 1.5 Grams
Fat: 4.8 Grams
Carbs: 21.9 Grams

Ingredients;

- 2 Cups Flour
- 1 ½ Cups Vegan Sugar
- 1 Teaspoon Baking Soda
- 1 Teaspoon Sea Salt, Fine
- ½ Cup Cocoa, Unsweetened
- 2 Tablespoons Vanilla Extract, Pure
- ½ Cup Oil
- 2 Cups Zucchini, Peeled & Grated

Directions:

1. Mix your cocoa, salt, flour, sugar and baking soda together.
2. Add in your oil, vanilla and zucchini, mixing well.
3. Bake at 350 in a nine by thirteen inch pan until done.

RADISH CHIPS

Serves: 4
Time: 20 Minutes
Calories: 3.6
Protein: 0.2 Grams
Fat: 0 Grams
Carbs: 0.8 Grams

Ingredients:

- 10-15 Radishes, Large
- Sea Salt & Black Pepper to Taste

Directions:

1. Start by heating your oven to 375.
2. Slice your radishes thin, and then spread them out on a cookie sheet that's been sprayed with cooking spray.
3. Mist the radishes with cooking spray, and then season with salt and pepper.
4. Bake for ten minutes, and then flip.
5. Bake for five to ten minutes more. They should be crispy.

SAUTÉED PEARS

Serves: 6
Time: 35 Minutes
Calories: 220
Protein: 2 Grams
Fat: 10 Grams
Carbs: 31 Grams

Ingredients:

- 2 Tablespoons Margarine (Or Vegan Butter)
- ¼ Teaspoon Cinnamon
- ¼ Teaspoon Nutmeg
- 6 Bosc Pears, Peeled & Quartered
- 1 Tablespoon Lemon Juice
- ½ Cup Walnuts, Toasted & Chopped (Optional)

Directions:

1. Melt your vegan butter in a skillet, and then add your spices. Cook for a half a minute before adding in your pears.
2. Cook for fifteen minutes, and then stir in your lemon juice.
3. Serve with walnuts if desired.

PUMPKIN & CINNAMON FUDGE

Serves: 25
Time: 2 Hours 10 Minutes
Calories: 110
Protein: 1.2 Grams
Fat: 10.63 Grams
Carbs: 5 Grams

Ingredients:

- 1 Teaspoon Ground Cinnamon
- 1 Cup Pumpkin Puree
- ¼ Teaspoon Nutmeg, Ground
- 1 ¾ Cup Coconut Butter, Melted
- 1 Tablespoon Coconut Oil

Directions:

1. Mix together your pumpkin, spices, coconut butter and coconut oil, whisking together.
2. Spread this mixture into a pan, and then cover it with foil. Press it down, and then discard the foil.
3. Refrigerate for two hours, and then chop into squares.

PECAN & BLUEBERRY CRUMBLE

Serves: 6
Time: 40 Minutes
Calories: 381
Protein: 10 Grams
Fat: 32 Grams
Net Carbs: 20 Grams

Ingredients:

- 14 Ounces Blueberries
- 1 Tablespoon Lemon Juice, Fresh
- 1 ½ Teaspoon Stevia Powder
- 3 Tablespoons Chia Seeds
- 2 Cups Almond Flour, Blanched
- ¼ Cup Pecans, Chopped
- 5 Tablespoon coconut Oil
- 2 Tablespoon Cinnamon

Directions:

1. Mix together your blueberries, stevia, chia seeds and lemon juice, and place it in an iron skillet.
2. Mix all remaining ingredients together in a bowl, spreading it over your blueberries.
3. Heat your oven to 400, and then transfer it to an oven safe skillet, baking for a half hour.

RICE PUDDING

Serves: 6
Time: 1 Hour 35 Minutes
Calories: 330
Protein: 5 Grams
Fat: 10 Grams
Carbs: 52 Grams

Ingredients:

- 1 Cup Brown Rice
- 1 Teaspoon Vanilla Extract, Pure
- ½ Teaspoon Sea Salt, Fine
- ½ Teaspoon Cinnamon
- ¼ Teaspoon Nutmeg
- 3 Egg Substitutes
- 3 Cups Coconut Milk, Light
- 2 Cups Brown Rice, Cooked

Directions:

1. Blend all of your ingredients together before pouring them into a two quarter dish.
2. Bake at 300 for ninety minutes before serving.

BLACK BEAN DIP

Serves: 2
Time: 10 Minutes
Calories: 190
Protein: 13 Grams
Fat: 1 Gram
Carbs: 35 Grams

Ingredients:

- 14 Ounces Black Beans, Drained & Rinsed
- 1 Lime, Juiced & Zested
- ¼ Cup Cilantro, Fresh & Chopped
- ¼ Cup Water
- 1 Teaspoon Cumin
- 1 Tablespoon Tamari
- Pinch Cayenne Pepper

Directions:

1. Process everything but your cilantro together until smooth, and then serve garnished with cilantro.

CONCLUSION

Now you have everything you need to get started making budget friendly, healthy plant-based recipes. Just follow your basic shopping list, and follow your meal plan to get started! It's easy to switch over to a plant-based diet if you have your meals planned out and temptation locked away. Don't forget to clean out your kitchen before starting, and you're sure to meet all your diet and health goals.

Start eating more fruits, vegetables, beans, whole grains, nuts, and seeds. Depending on how far you want to take it, you can cut back on animal products, or cut them out.

Like any diet, the health benefits are dependent on the quality and _nutritional adequacy_ of the diet – this means replacing refined, typically 'white' carbohydrates with wholegrains, avoiding sugary, sweetened drinks and confectionery and focusing on good quality plant-based protein and fats, such as those found in nuts and seeds. Follow my plant-based diet meal plan and be ready to cook some amazing recipes that can help you to stay healthy.

Wish you good luck with plant-based diet!

Manufactured by
Amazon.ca
Bolton, ON